HOT MOMS Cookbook®

Hot Moms CookBook®

Created by: Sandro & Daniela
Design by: 2Gen.Net

Published by Hot Moms CookBook®

Printed in China 2014

www.hotmomscookbook.com
www.hotmomscooking.com

ISBN 978-0-9878265-0-3

PHOTOGRAPHY BY TANYA SMITH

www.tanyaLsmith.com

My name is Tanya, I am the owner and photographer at Tanya Smith Photography, located just west of Toronto, Ontario Canada. I have been a photographer for the past 10 years.

Photographing everything from corporate events, to food to portraits and verything in between. When I met Sandro and Daniela and heard about their idea of creating a cookbook of real life moms recipes, I couldn't resist. I had so much fun shooting all the yummy dishes for this book and hope you enjoy it!

t

Hot
Hot

THE MOMS

THIS BOOK IS DEDICATED TO ALL MOMS

You walk through the door
Not a clue what to make
Sauté, fry, broil or bake

Leave everything raw and crude
Cook in your new apron or even in the nude
Dice a tomato round and red
Toss in some greens or a cucumber instead
No kidding, no messing
Don't forget the salad dressing

The ingredients read:

Stir in some rice, add some flour
Shake in spice and cook for an hour
Don't be afraid, turn a new leaf
Add some potatoes and a slice of beef

Make a soup, make a stew
Make it with love, it comes from you
Try your hardest and be your best
If not for you, at least for your guest

Pick up a spoon, pick up this book
Stare at the moon and start to cook
Things may get hectic, try to stay calm
Because at the end of it all, you're still a mom

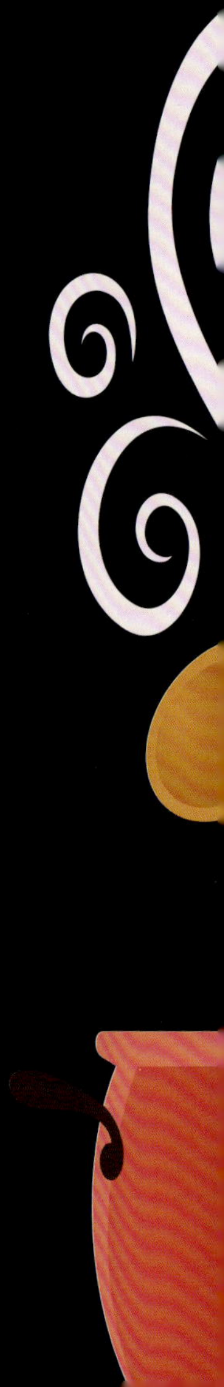

A SPECIAL PREFACE

Forget about celebrity chefs and all the big name cookbooks and food gurus with their couscous and tar tar. Oh please, these mothers never went to culinary school, nor did they have fancy ingredients in which I could never find at my local supermarket anyway. These Real Moms simply opened up their fridge and cooked real food. Most of these moms didn't even have their recipes written down as we watched in amazement how simple it was to cook.

Thank you to all the moms who shared their kitchen with us, and prepared these nutritional, easy and delicious homemade meals your whole family will enjoy!

ALYSSA

Alyssa is a professional harpist, teacher, recording artist and adjudicator. After graduating with a Master's in Harp performance, Alyssa started a private music business. As well as teaching private harp and piano lessons, she also teaches harp at the University of Western Ontario. Her other positions include adjudicating for the Royal Conservatory of Canada as well as Kiwanis festivals and Harp Society competitions. She is known for being one of the most active performing modern harpists providing electric harp entertainment to clients all over Ontario, blending classical sounds and techniques with her uniquely stylized arrangements of contemporary music.

Borscht is known as the chicken soup of Eastern Europe. This authentic Ukrainian recipe was passed down to me by my grandmother Myra. Every time we came over for dinner, borscht was on the menu. It was hard not to have three bowls full before the main course even came out! Before Myra passed away, we spent a week in her kitchen cooking many of her famous recipes while I watched, took notes and helped her cook. Every time I make it, I'm reminded of my fond childhood memories cooking with my grandmother.

UKRANIAN BORSCHT

PREP 25 mins

COOK 15 mins

SERVES 6

INGREDIENTS

- ☐ 1/8 head cabbage
- ☐ 3 medium carrots
- ☐ 2 celery stalks
- ☐ 3 large beets, grated
- ☐ 1 onion
- ☐ 4 large tomatoes
- ☐ 1/2 cup green beans, chopped (or white beans)
- ☐ 3/4 cup little pasta (mini shells, macaroni, etc.)
- ☐ 1 small potato, chopped
- ☐ 1/2 green pepper, chopped
- ☐ 3 cups beef broth
- ☐ 3 cups chicken broth
- ☐ 3 cups beet water
- ☐ 2 tablespoons lemon juice
- ☐ 2 tablespoons butter
- ☐ 1 tablespoon canola oil

1 Wash beets skin on.

2 Boil beets skin on.

3 When cooked, peel and grate (either with cheese grater or food processor).

4 Be sure to wear gloves if doing this by hand!

5 Save beet water.

6 Cook tomatoes whole covering with water.

Besides having over 80 different nutrients that our body needs, beets were often used for dyes and colouring in the Medieval and Renaissance period. Remember, if you are grating the beets by hand, use a bag or a pair of plastic gloves to cover your hands!

7 In a large pot, cook all the chopped vegetables in butter and oil.

Most recipes use potatoes as the starch in the soup, however, my grandmother would always add pasta t our soup to make it more enticing for the kids to ea I actually prefer the little shells over potatoes, but f free to add both or neithe

8

Add beef and chicken broth, 3 cups of the beet water and lemon juice.

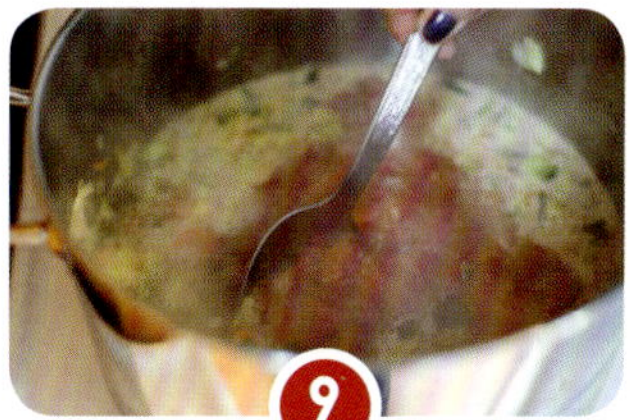

9

Peel and strain tomatoes into pot.

10

Bring to a boil and add grated beets and pasta. Reduce to medium and cook.

11

Add salt and pepper and chopped green peppers.

For an alternate version of this soup, try blending the ingredients into a smooth puree. This is a great way to "disguise" the ingredients from our little picky eaters (and sometimes the big ones too!)

Sour cream is the most common additive at the end, but sometimes for an even richer treat, I like to add half and half cream!

MAMA'S MEAT PATTIES

PREP 20 mins

COOK 40 mins

SERVES 6

INGREDIENTS

- ☐ 1 cup dry bread crumbs
- ☐ 1 cup milk or more
- ☐ 1/2 pound ground veal
- ☐ 1/2 pound ground beef
- ☐ 1/2 pound ground pork
- ☐ 1 small onion, grated
- ☐ 1 egg, slightly beaten
- ☐ Salt and pepper
- ☐ Sifted dry bread crumbs
- ☐ Butter

INSTRUCTIONS

1. Put the bread crumbs into a large bowl and add the milk on top. Let stand for a few minutes.
2. Add remaining ingredients except for sifted bread crumbs and butter. Mix thoroughly by hand.
3. Season with salt and pepper.
4. Shape into round thick patties and dip into bread crumbs.
5. In a pan, brown both sides of patty in hot butter.
6. Do not cook to many patties at once - they should not be overcrowded in pan.
7. Remove partially cooked patties and place in baking dish while browning the rest.
8. When all are complete, cover baking dish and place in oven to complete cooking - about 25 minutes at 350°F.
9. Serve immediately while warm with a creamed mushroom sauce or the like.

PAPA'S POTATO PANCAKES

PREP 10 mins

COOK 10 mins

SERVES 8-10

INGREDIENTS

- 2 eggs
- 1/2 an onion
- 1 teaspoon salt
- 1/4 cup flour
- 1/4 teaspoon baking powder
- 2 cups raw potato, cubed

INSTRUCTIONS

Place all ingredients inside a blender in the order listed.

Cover and process at low speed.

Stop blender and scrape down sides with rubber spatula.

Do not over blend! Pour batter onto a hot, well greased griddle.

Using bacon fat grease is delicious!

Brown on both sides.

Drain on absorbent paper.

Serve hot and fresh with sour cream on top.

ANGIE

Being of Italian origin, our lives revolve around family, friends and especially food. Cooking for my husband, my boys and many friends & family who come through the front door brings such joy. My home is always open; with a revolving door, greeting and hosting is second nature.

There is so much love and respect around the kitchen table which keeps a family strong and united, and there is nothing my boys love more than seeing their mama cooking their favourite meals.

Being a self-employed medical aesthetician by profession and practising for over 15 years, I have established a connection with my clients, gaining their trust and providing dedication and attention to their personal needs has given me reign.

When career and passion for life come together, along with a supportive family you cannot but reward your loved ones, and there is no better satisfaction than food!

SICILIAN KISS MEATZZA

PREP 15 mins

COOK 35 mins

SERVES 6

INGREDIENTS

- ☐ 1 pizza dough
- ☐ 250 grams each ground pork, veal & beef
- ☐ 1 head cauliflower
- ☐ 1 cup kalamata olives
- ☐ 15 anchovies
- ☐ 1 bunch scallions
- ☐ 500 grams ricotta cheese
- ☐ 5 fresh hot chili peppers
- ☐ Sea salt
- ☐ Black pepper
- ☐ Olive oil

1

Begin by spreading out the pizza dough into a rectangular shape. Brush a light coating of olive oil over the pizza dough. Combine the ground beef, veal and pork.

2

Season with salt and black pepper.

3

Chop cauliflower into small pieces.

4

Chop up anchovies & chilli peppers.

5

Remove pit from kalamata olives & divide each olive in half.

6

Chop up scallions.

7

Spread ricotta cheese evenly over the dough. Then spread the chili peppers, anchovies, scallions and kalamata olives evenly.

8

Gently roll the dough with all its ingredients into a roll.

9

Slice each roll into 1-inch pieces.

10

Gently twist and compress each piece (circle) and place on a greased baking sheet about 2½-inches apart.

11

Bake at 450°F for 35 minutes.

LEMON BUTTER SCALLOPS

PREP 20 mins

COOK 40 mins

SERVES 6

INGREDIENTS

- ☐ 12 large fresh scallops
- ☐ 50 grams butter
- ☐ Juice from 1/2 lemon
- ☐ 1 tablespoon parsley, chopped
- ☐ 2 tablespoons fish stock
- ☐ Salt and pepper
- ☐ Flour for dusting

INSTRUCTIONS

1. Dust the scallops lightly with the flour.
2. Heat butter in a large pan and add the scallops and fry for 2 minutes on each side.
3. Remove the scallops from the pan and place on a side dish.
4. Add fish stock and lemon juice to the pan, stirring well. If necessary, add a little more stock for more juice if required.
5. Add parsley and salt and pepper, stir well.
6. Return the scallops to the pan, let them heat through then serve at once, pouring a little juice over each portion.

COZY PASTA E FAGIOLI

PREP 10 mins

COOK 35 mins

SERVES 3-4

INGREDIENTS

- ☐ 1 tablespoon olive oil
- ☐ 1 medium onion, diced
- ☐ 1 celery stalk, diced
- ☐ 3 cloves garlic, minced
- ☐ 1 can tomato sauce
- ☐ 3 cups chicken broth
- ☐ 1/2 cup parmesan cheese, grated
- ☐ 1 can cannellini beans, drained (white kidney beans)
- ☐ Salt and pepper
- ☐ 1/2 tablespoon dried oregano
- ☐ 1/2 tablespoon dried parsley
- ☐ 3 fresh basil leaves
- ☐ 1 cup any small dried pasta

INSTRUCTIONS

1. In a large deep pot with olive oil, saute onion, garlic, and celery.
2. Season with salt and pepper.
3. Add tomato sauce, beans, broth, oregano and parsley.
4. Cover and let mixture come to a boil, then add the basil.
5. Heat to a boil. Reduce heat to medium-low; cover and simmer 10 minutes, stirring occasionally.
6. Remove cover; increase to high heat and bring to a boil.
7. Reduce heat to medium. Add pasta; cook 10 to 15 minutes or until al dente.
8. Add parmesan separately.

ANTONIETTA

J'aime cuisiner et manger de la nourriture saine et végétarienne. (any guess as to what that means? Hint: J'aime= I like / cuisiner= to cook / manger= to eat / nourriture= food / saine= healthy)

Eating healthy and staying fit gives me the strength I need to be who I am. I am eager to learn, courageous to try and too stubborn to ever give up. My children keep me feeling young and have helped me to become more patient. I love teaching my high-school students French because it gives me the opportunity to talk about culture, music and art. My students, who sit in my Food and Nutrition course that I also teach, hear me speak passionately about caring for our health, choosing healthy foods especially those that grow on a tree or come from the ground and to occasionally splurge on foods that give us comfort. I love this topic so much that I decided to pursue it further and enrolled in a two year diploma program that gives me the opportunity to be a Holistic Nutritionist. By the time you read this, I will be ready and excited to share my wealth of knowledge.

VEGETARIAN STUFFED LENTIL EGGPLANTS

PREP 30 mins

COOK 25 mins

SERVES 4

INGREDIENTS

- ☐ 1/2 yellow onion
- ☐ 1 can crushed tomatoes
- ☐ 1 can tomato paste
- ☐ 1 cup water
- ☐ 2 cups cooked brown rice
- ☐ 1 can corn
- ☐ 1 can lentils
- ☐ 2 cups mozzarella cheese, shredded
- ☐ 2 large eggplants
- ☐ 1 tablespoon garlic powder
- ☐ 1 tablespoon oregano
- ☐ 1 tablespoon parsley
- ☐ 3/4 cup olive or vegetable oil
- ☐ 2 tablespoons salt
- ☐ 1/2 cup parmesan cheese, grated

1

Chop half an onion. Add to a big pot with a few drizzles of olive/vegetable oil. Cook the onion on medium heat until they are slightly brown. Add the crushed tomatoes and tomato paste to the onions with one cup of water.

2

Stir then add the spices and salt. Let cook on medium to low heat for half hour.

3

Prepare the rice according to the directions on the package. Once cooked, place in a bowl and sprinkle a bit of the spices.

4

Rinse the corn and the lentils.

5

Add the corn and lentils to the rice. Sprinkle with the remainder of the spices but leave some salt for step #9.

Eggplants are low in calories, with just 35 per cup. It contains no fat and its high fiber content can help you feel full.

6

Add some olive oil just so that the ric looks moistened.

7

Add the mozzarella cheese to the mixture and stir.

TIP You can use the remainder of the tomato sauce for another meal or freeze it.

8

Slice each eggplant in half lengthwise.

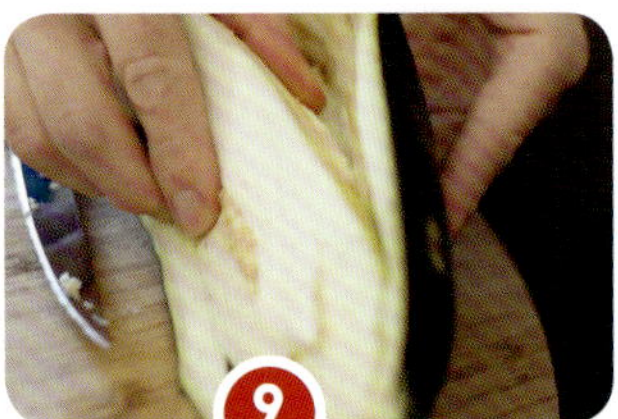

9

Spoon out most of the pulp from each half of the eggplant so that the eggplant has room for the rice filling. Place some of the olive oil in your hands and lather the outside and inside of each eggplant. Sprinkle salt inside the eggplant.

10

Add the rice mixture in the eggplant and press down with a fork.

11

Add tomato sauce over each eggplant. Sprinkle the parmesan cheese on the eggplants.

Place the eggplants on a baking sheet and bake in oven at 325°F for about 25 minutes or when the eggplant feels soft.

12

CHEEKY CHICKPEA SOUP

PREP 15 mins

COOK 30 mins

SERVES 4

INGREDIENTS

- ☐ 1/2 yellow onion, chopped
- ☐ 1 clove garlic, crushed
- ☐ 2 tablespoons of tomato sauce
- ☐ 2 carrots, chopped
- ☐ 1 can chickpeas
- ☐ 1 tablespoon olive oil
- ☐ 1/4 teaspoon salt
- ☐ 1/4 teaspoon oregano
- ☐ 1/2 -1 cup water

INSTRUCTIONS

1. Cook the chopped onion and garlic in a saucepan with the olive oil until the onions brown.
2. Add the chopped carrots and cook on medium heat for about 3 minutes.
3. Add half the water and the tomato sauce and cook on medium to low heat for about 10 minutes.
4. Add the chickpeas to the saucepan with the rest of the water. Then add the salt and oregano.
5. Stir then cover on low heat for about 15 to 20 minutes.

CHOCOLATE BEAN BROWNIES

PREP 10 mins

COOK 35 mins

SERVES 4

INGREDIENTS

- ☐ 1½ cups canned black beans (drained, rinsed and mashed)
- ☐ 1/4 cup whole wheat flour
- ☐ 1/2 cup unsweetened cocoa powder
- ☐ 1 teaspoon baking powder
- ☐ 1/2 teaspoon salt
- ☐ 3 large eggs
- ☐ 1 cup granulated sugar
- ☐ 1/2 cup applesauce
- ☐ 4 tablespoons canola oil
- ☐ 2 teaspoons vanilla
- ☐ 1/4 cup miniature semi-sweet chocolate chips

INSTRUCTIONS

1. Preheat oven to 350°F.
2. Line an 8-inch square metal baking pan with foil, leaving some overhang at opposite ends.
3. Lightly spray foil with non-stick cooking spray.
4. In a large bowl, combine the beans, flour, cocoa powder, baking powder and salt.
5. With a wooden spoon, beat in eggs, sugar, applesauce, oil and vanilla until mixed well.
6. Stir in chocolate chips.
7. Pour batter in baking dish.
8. Bake for 30 to 35 minutes or until toothpick inserted in the centre comes out clean.
9. Remove from pan, transfer to cutting board and slice to your delight.

CYNTHIA & ISABELLE

Cynthia

I began my career as a flight attendant, caring for people with the comfort of reassurance and know-how aboard each flight. Several years later I became a stay at home mom, caring for my two children. Although this break from the workforce was somewhat short lived, spending the time with my family was time well spent. Now juggling a household and a career prove challenging at times, I never loose sight of how important family and friends are, I always find the time to indulge in social gatherings, also contributing to the preservation of living a lasting, meaningful and well fulfilled life.

Isabelle

As the founder of a full service design studio business, I have acquired a wealth of experience in managing, creating and delivering small to large scale projects. My strong understanding of business and people guides my positive and fresh approach to problem solving. Along with this career, coincides my personal life passions (to name a few), including travelling, and indulging in precious moments with family and friends.

This brings us to the kitchen, where a majority of gatherings tend to converge; creating dishes that seemingly increase the pallets temptation with each new recipe achieved. This passion for creating food that not only nourishes, but develops a warm inviting experience is most likely influenced by our French Canadian background. We realized, not only were we sisters, but also best friends. "Cooking, baking and preparing great food for everyone that we hold dear, is the most therapeutic thing we could do."

Hot
Mom
Cooking
Hot
Mom

MUCHO BEEF BURRITOS

PREP 20 mins

COOK 3.5 hours

SERVES 6

INGREDIENTS

- ☐ Blade roast
- ☐ 4 cups beef broth
- ☐ 4 cloves of garlic
- ☐ 2 bay leaves
- ☐ 1 tablespoon of Worcestershire sauce
- ☐ 1 tablespoon of peppercorns
- ☐ 1 tall can of dark ale
- ☐ 2 large carrots and celery, chopped
- ☐ 2 cups cooked brown rice
- ☐ 1/2 pack taco seasoning mix
- ☐ 1 onion, chopped
- ☐ 1 red and 1 yellow pepper, diced
- ☐ 1 jalapeno, diced and seeded
- ☐ 1 cup salsa and 1 cup sour cream
- ☐ 1/2 cup black beans, drained
- ☐ 1/2 cup parsley, chopped
- ☐ 1 cup cheddar cheese, grated
- ☐ 6 large flour tortillas

1

Start your oven at 350°F.
In a cast iron dutch oven add blade roast, beef broth, garlic, bay leaves, Worcestershire sauce, peppercorns, ale, carrots and celery. Place in oven up to 3 to 4 hours.

2

Once blade roast is easy to pull apart it is ready. Remove from oven set aside to rest (this step can be done ahead of time).

3

Pull roast apart and place in a container ready to be used.

4

Cook brown rice as per packaging (when cooking rice add ½ taco seasoning mix).

Bell peppers should be stored unwashed, in the vegetable compartment of the refrigerator. If stored correctly, they will keep fresh for up to a week. Bell peppers may also be frozen. Store whole peppers in an airtight, freezer-safe container.

Add chopped jalapeno, parsley, red and yellow diced pepper to the rice bowl.

Add drained black beans to the rice bowl.

Add onions.

8

Place 1 flour tortilla on a plate add 3/4 cup of rice mixture then add 1/2 cup of pulled roast on top.

9

Add grated cheese and parsley.

10

Roll the tortilla, secure with a toothpick and place in a rectangular 4x6 roasting pan. Once you have placed the 6 tortillas in the roasting pan put in the oven at 375°F for 20 to 30 minutes until crispy to the touch.
Serve with salsa and sour cream.

STUFFED PINATA JALAPENOS & MUSHROOMS

PREP 30 mins
COOK 25 mins
SERVES 24

INGREDIENTS

- ☐ 12 jalapenos
- ☐ 12 white mushrooms
- ☐ 1/2 medium onion, finely diced
- ☐ 4 cloves of garlic, finely minced
- ☐ 8 ounces cream cheese
- ☐ 1 egg
- ☐ 3/4 cup parmesan cheese, grated
- ☐ 1/3 cup dry white wine
- ☐ Salt and pepper to taste
- ☐ 1/3 pound hot pork sausage

Remove sausage from casing. In a frying pan on medium heat, crumble and brown sausage. Set aside on a plate to cool.

Add onions and garlic to the same skillet, cook for 2 minutes over medium to low heat. Pour in wine to de glaze the pan and allow the liquid to evaporate.

Separate mushroom caps from stems set aside caps for stuffing, and chop mushroom stems for mixture.

Add in chopped mushroom stems, stir to cook for 2 minutes. Add salt and pepper to taste. Set mixture aside on a plate to cool.

5

In a mixing bowl, combine cream cheese and egg yolk. Stir together with parmesan cheese.

6

Add cooled sausage and cooled mushrooms stems. Stir mixture together and refrigerate for a short time to firm up.

TIP Allow to cool at least ten minutes before serving, tastes better when not piping hot.

7

Slice jalapenos length wise in half.

8

Add meat mixture into the cavity of each jalapeno and mushroom cap, creating a sizable mound over the top.

9

Bake at 350°F for 20 to 25 minutes, or until golden brown.

HUEVOS RANCHEROS BREAKFAST

PREP 10 mins

COOK 20 mins

SERVES 2

INGREDIENTS

- ☐ 3 tablespoons vegetable oil
- ☐ 1 medium onion, chopped
- ☐ 1 clove garlic, finely chopped
- ☐ Chili peppers, chopped, to taste
- ☐ 1 pinch chili powder
- ☐ 4 plum tomatoes, peeled, seeded and chopped
- ☐ 2 corn tortillas
- ☐ 2 eggs
- ☐ 1/2 teaspoon sugar
- ☐ Salt and pepper, to taste
- ☐ 1 tablespoon cilantro or pars finely chopped

INSTRUCTIONS

1. To prepare the ranchero sauce, in a skillet, heat 1 tablespoon oil over medium to high heat.
2. Add onion and garlic, and saute until softened but not brown, 4 to 5 minutes.
3. Add tomatoes, peppers, chili powder, salt and black pepper and reduce to a simmer. Simmer for about 10 minutes, until the sauce begins to thicken.
4. Add cilantro or parsley, turn off the heat and cover the pan to keep the sauce warm.
5. In another skillet, lightly fry the tortillas in 1 tablespoon of oil. Remove and drain.
6. If necessary, add additional oil to the second skillet, and fry the eggs until they are "sunny-side up." Transfer the eggs to the tortillas, and cover with the ranchero sauce.

ENTICING MEATLOAF

PREP 10 mins

COOK 60 mins

SERVES 4-6

INGREDIENTS

- ☐ 1½ pounds ground beef
- ☐ 1 cup round crackers
- ☐ 2 beaten eggs
- ☐ 1 cup tomato sauce
- ☐ 1/2 cup onion
- ☐ 1/2 teaspoon salt
- ☐ 1/4 teaspoon pepper

INSTRUCTIONS

1. Preheat the oven to 350°F.
2. Pound the crackers until fine like bread crumbs.
3. Mince the onion finely.
4. In a separate bowl, add the meat and the other ingredients and mix with your hands until the ingredients are all mixed together and the mixture is smooth.
5. Grease a glass baking pan with vegetable shortening.
6. Put the meat mixture in the pan and shape like a football.
7. Bake in the oven for 1 hour.
8. Take out the meat loaf and serve warm.

DANIELA

As a proud mom of two girls, I have been a stay-at-home mom since my first angel was born. I volunteer my time with various charities and at my daughter's school as a parent representative on the school council.

Although I am not the greatest chef, cooking for a creative man seems challenging at times, I try my hardest to make easy meals that my family will enjoy. However, baking on the other hand is definitely one of my strengths; hence my main recipe was Tiramisu, which means, "pick me up" in Italian.

Depending on how much vermouth you add, you could truly make this dessert a pick me upper.

hotmomcooking.com

PICK ME UP A... TIRAMISU

PREP 15 mins

COOK 3-4 hours

SERVES 10

INGREDIENTS

- ☐ 2 cups espresso coffee
- ☐ 1/3 cup sweet Italian vermouth
- ☐ 40 lady finger cookies (approximately)
- ☐ 500 grams fresh mascarpone cheese
- ☐ 5 eggs
- ☐ 5 tablespoons sugar
- ☐ Bittersweet chocolate for shaving or cinnamon

1

Brew espresso, in another bowl, mix together espresso and vermouth.

2

Separate the yolks from the whites into two different mixing bowls.

3

In the bowl with the yolks, add sugar and beat yolk mixture with an electric mixer until consistency is creamy.

4

Add mascarpone cheese and mix thoroughly.

5

In the other mixing bowl, beat egg whites until th
turn into fluffy white peaks. Carefully fold egg wh
into the creamy yolk mixture.

6

cookies in coffee mixture for a few seconds, making sure they are wet ide but still somewhat dry in the middle. Arrange dipped cookies in one tly packed layer on the bottom of an 8′ or 9′ springform pan, leaving a ch gap between the sides and the ladyfingers. The 1-inch gap is so you can add the ladyfingers in an upright position.

7

Place ladyfingers, in upright position, sugar side out, against the pan. Be sure to push them into the dipped cookies on the bottom of the springform pan and fit them tightly against one another. Pour 1/2 of the cream on top of the cookies and spread evenly.

8

econd layer of soaked lady fingers, then evenly spread the remaining cream Continue the process until all the cream mixture is finished and is the top layer of the tiramisu.

9

Leave tiramisu to rest in the fridge for 3 to 4 hours or overnight. Before serving, sprinkle with chocolate shavings or cinnamon.

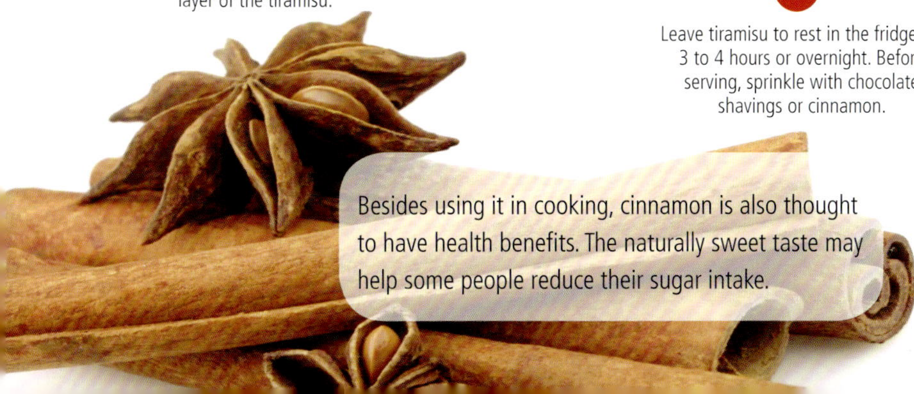

Besides using it in cooking, cinnamon is also thought to have health benefits. The naturally sweet taste may help some people reduce their sugar intake.

LEAN MEAN PORK CHOPS MUSHROOM GRAVY

PREP 15 mins
COOK 90 mins
SERVES 6

INGREDIENTS

- ☐ 6 pork chops (do not use fast-fry pork chops)
- ☐ 1 teaspoon salt
- ☐ 1 - 2 teaspoons garlic powder
- ☐ 2 large eggs, beaten
- ☐ 1/3 cup all-purpose flour
- ☐ 2 cups seasoned dry bread crumbs
- ☐ 2 tablespoons butter

MUSHROOM GRAVY

- ☐ 2 cans cream mushroom soup, undiluted
- ☐ 1 can sliced mushrooms, well drained
- ☐ 3/4 cup milk
- ☐ 1/3 cup dry white wine (can use a few tablespoons more)
- ☐ 1/2 teaspoon fresh ground black pepper
- ☐ 1 pinch cayenne pepper (optional)
- ☐ 1/3 cup parmesan cheese, grated (optional)

INSTRUCTIONS

1. Grease a 13x9 inch baking dish.
2. Pat the pork chops dry using paper towels, then season with salt, pepper and garlic powder.
3. Place the eggs in a bowl, then flour in another bowl and the bread crumbs in another bowl.
4. Heat oil and butter in a skillet over medium heat.
5. Dredge the pork chops first in flour then in eggs allowing any excess egg to drip off.
6. Coat in seasoned bread crumbs.
7. Brown the pork chops in hot oil about 4 to 5 minutes per side or until the breading is light golden brown.
8. Transfer the chops to a baking dish.
9. Cover with foil.
10. Set oven to 350°F and bake for about 1 hour.
11. Meanwhile, in a bowl combine cream of mushroom soup with sliced mushrooms, milk, white wine, black pepper and cayenne pepper, (if using).
12. After 1 hour baking pour the mushroom gravy over the pork chops, then sprinkle with grated parmesan cheese.
13. Replace the foil and bake for another 25 to 30 minutes or until chops are tender.
14. May be served with mashed potatoes and peas.

RISQUE RISOTTO MILANESE

PREP 15 mins

COOK 30 mins

SERVES 6

INGREDIENTS

- ☐ 1 small onion, finely chopped
- ☐ 2 teaspoons olive oil
- ☐ 400 grams aborio rice
- ☐ 3 litres hot stock (vegetable or meat)
- ☐ 2 teaspoons saffron powder or 1 teaspoon saffron strands
- ☐ Sea salt, to taste
- ☐ 1 tablespoon butter
- ☐ 1/2 cup parmesan cheese, grated

INSTRUCTIONS

1. In a large, deep saucepan over medium to low heat, fry the onion in the heated olive oil until transparent.
2. Add the rice and stir to coat well. Add the hot stock, one ladle at a time, allowing the liquid to be absorbed after each addition and stirring frequently.
3. Continue in this way until the rice is tender and falls off a spoon heavily - this should take approximately 20 minutes.
4. Add the saffron and season with salt. If desired, stir in a large tablespoon of butter, then serve scattered with a generous handful of grated parmesan cheese.

DARLENE

Affectionately known as Dee, I love being a mom and enjoy preparing a hearty home cooked meal for my baby girls and my husband. Being married to a Jamaican, and also a Jamaican citizen myself, I am very influenced by the West Indian culture and find many of my favourite foods being of Caribbean origin. The recipe I provided, "Escovitch Fish", is a traditional Jamaican dish, normally served with, rice and beans (rice made with coconut milk and red kidney beans), or a flat bread made from Cassava called "Bammy."

Every time we go to Jamaica, my husband has to take me to my favourite spot on the island. It is called "Border." This is where I fell in love with Escovitch Fish. The fish there is caught fresh each day and you have about thirty to forty vendors on the side of the street in their little shops, all selling fish and bammy. It's not just great food, it's an experience.

JAMAICAN ESCOVITCH FISH WITH RICE & BEANS

PREP 30 mins

COOK 30 mins

SERVES 4

INGREDIENTS

- ☐ 4 red snapper fish (scaled & cleaned)
- ☐ 2 limes
- ☐ 1 cup vegetable oil
- ☐ 1 cup dry kidney beans
- ☐ 1 can coconut milk
- ☐ 1 cup water
- ☐ 2 cloves garlic, chopped
- ☐ 2 stalks scallions, chopped
- ☐ 1 teaspoon dried thyme
- ☐ 1½ teaspoons salt, to taste
- ☐ 1 teaspoon black pepper
- ☐ 2 cups long grain rice (rinsed and drained)
- ☐ 1 tablespoon butter
- ☐ Fish seasoning

Sauce

- ☐ 1 cup vinegar
- ☐ 4 pinches all spice
- ☐ 2 large onions
- ☐ 3 carrots
- ☐ 1 green pepper
- ☐ 2 scotch bonnet peppers
- ☐ Pinch of salt
- ☐ 1 teaspoon white sugar

1

Boil the beans in a pot of water, about 4 cups water until the beans are soft. Approximately an hour.

2

Once the beans are cooked, the beans would have soaked up half the water, you can now add your can of coconut milk, and gauge if you need to add more water. It should look like about 4 cups of liquid.

3

Now add thyme, 1 tablespoon butter, green onion, salt, pepper, and a scotch bonnet if you like, whole.

Bring to a boil on high and then cover and reduce to low and simmer until all liquid is absorbed and rice is cooked. Fluff with a fork.

4

Take a knife and run it over the fish to check for any left over scales while under cool water, once nice and smooth, you are ready.

Take your limes cut in half to squeeze over the fish, which is great to get rid of the rawness from the fish and give it a nice clean. You can use lime juice if you do not have fresh limes, or even vinegar.

Rinse with cool water and pat dry. Then using a sharp knife cut a couple slits across the belly of the fish (both sides), this will allow for faster cooking and to help the salt and black pepper as well as the escovitch sauce to really infuse the fish.

Season your fish with salt, black pepper and your choice of fish seasoning rubbing it onto the fish (both sides) and get ready to fry.

5

Heat the vegetable oil on medium heat, then gently add the seasoned fish to the pan. Allow to cook for 4 to 5 minutes on each side, or until you have a nice golden color and crisp outside.

The oil can splatter so be careful and use long tongs to flip the fish. Remove from the pan and place on paper towels to soak up some of the excess oil and set aside while you prepare the Escovitch sauce.

6 Place all ingredients for the sauce including vinegar, sugar, all spice, julienne carrots, sweet pepper, sliced onion, scotch bonnet, salt and pepper and add to sauce pan.

7 Using medium heat, bring to a gentle simmer. Allow this to simmer for 3 to 5 minutes, basically until the onion and sweet pepper (bell pepper) gets a bit tender. Depending on how you like your veggies, a bit crisp cook for 3 minutes, 5 minutes for softer veggies. I like my sauce with a bit of crunch so I cooked it for 3 minutes, you can cook for longer if you wish. You can make your sauce up to 2 weeks prior, the longer it sits the more it pickles, which is even tastier.

Now plate your fish and place a hearty spoonful of sauce along the top. Then scoop a cup of rice and beans as your side dish.

SPECIAL VANILLA CREPES

PREP 20 mins

COOK 40 mins

SERVES 6

INGREDIENTS

- ☐ 1 cup milk
- ☐ 1 cup all purpose flour
- ☐ 2 eggs
- ☐ 1/2 teaspoon vanilla extract
- ☐ 1/2 teaspoon salt
- ☐ 1 teaspoon of oil

INSTRUCTIONS

1. Mix flour and salt together then add milk, eggs and vanilla.
2. Using a mixer or by hand, you want the consistency to be on the thinner side.
3. Add a teaspoon of oil, and use a ladle to pour your first crepe into the pan, you take the handle of the frying pan, (with a oven mitt if hot) and swirl your pan around to make a thin round crepe. Do this on medium heat, and flip once the top side shows signs of bubbles.
4. If you are quick, you can have 2 frying pans going at the same time.
5. You can put them on a plate and keep them warm in the oven at 200°F until done, or like in my family, we eat them on the fly, I have a line up behind me and just keep plating them! Makes about 6 to 8 crepes depending on size.

HOMEMADE SALAD UNDRESSING

PREP 10 mins

COOK 10 mins

SERVES 4

INGREDIENTS

- ☐ 1 cup olive oil
- ☐ 1/3 cup balsamic vinegar (or a Herbal or Rice Wine)
- ☐ 1 teaspoon sugar (I use organic cane sugar)
- ☐ 1/2 teaspoon salt
- ☐ 1/2 teaspoon ground black pepper (or white)
- ☐ 3 cloves garlic, pressed/crushed (or however many you like)

INSTRUCTIONS

1. Place all ingredients in a mixing cup, shake and enjoy! Stays in the fridge for a few weeks. The oil will harden, so take it out a little while prior to using it to come to room temperature. So great not only on salad, but on mixed and grilled veggies!

JOANNE

It gives me great pleasure in my life ensuring that all those around me share in my zest for life as well as allowing me to make them feel special in their own way. While raising 3 wonderful children and balancing a very successful career, I also get great satisfaction from the time I dedicate to serving a variety of different charities including raising money for the homeless through, "Hockey Helps the Homeless," Kelly Shires Breast Cancer Foundation, numerous Hospital for Sick Children fundraising events and I am involved in a handful of other charities. I feel that my drive, hard work, positive attitude and desire to help all those around me allows me to be considered a good role model for my children. I work hard on keeping myself healthy and in shape, so I know that you will enjoy my Wild Banana Muffins recipe, (especially if you use the rice flour as a gluten free recipe). I hope that you enjoy this recipe as much as my family and friends have.

Happy Baking!

Hot
Mom
Cooking
hotmomcooking.com

WILD BANANA MUFFINS

PREP 15 mins

COOK 30 mins

SERVES 24

INGREDIENTS

- ☐ 3-4 ripe bananas
- ☐ 3/4 cup sugar
- ☐ 1 egg
- ☐ 1 teaspoon vanilla
- ☐ 1/2 cup margarine
- ☐ 1 teaspoon salt
- ☐ 1 teaspoon baking soda
- ☐ 1½ cups flour
- ☐ 1 heaping teaspoon baking powder
- ☐ Brown sugar
- ☐ Cinnamon
- ☐ Chocolate chips

1

Place ripe bananas in food processor and reduce to mushy bananas.

2

Add sugar, egg, vanilla and blend. Then add margarine, salt and baking soda and mix again.

3

Add flour and mix until all flour has been mixed well. Finally, add baking powder, but do not mix for more than 20 seconds.

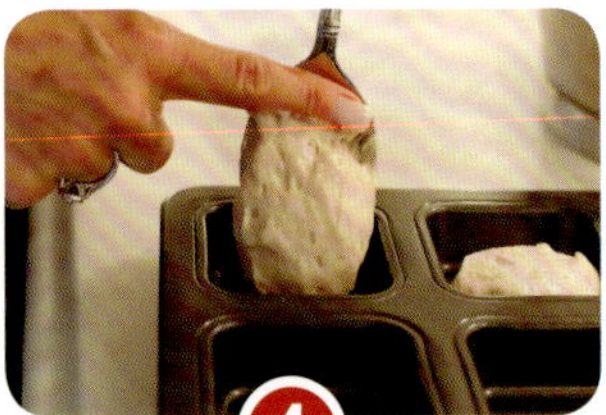

4

Place dough in each cup enough to fill 2/3 of the muffin pan.

5

Sprinkle a little cinnamon.

6

Add some brown sugar.

7

Top with chocolate chips.

8

Place on middle rack for 20 minutes at 350°F. Top of muffins should be golden to light brown in color.

AMORE AMARETTO COOKIES

PREP 5 mins

COOK 10 mins

SERVES 24

INGREDIENTS

- ☐ 2 eggs
- ☐ 1 cup sugar
- ☐ 1/2 teaspoon cocoa powder
- ☐ 4 teaspoons almond extract
- ☐ 3 cups almonds, crushed

INSTRUCTIONS

1. Place the whole almonds in the food processor to create crushed almonds.
2. Add sugar and blend.
3. Add cocoa powder and blend.
4. Add eggs and almond extract, turn on food processor until it won't mix anymore.
5. Empty into a large bowl and finish mixing all of the ingredients by hand.
6. Add a little butter to the palm of your hand and rub your hands together. This will prevent the cookie dough from sticking to them when you work with the dough.
7. Take a small portion of cookie dough and roll it in your hands to create a ball.
8. Place on cookie sheet leaving approximately 3-inches between.
9. Add a full almond to the top of each cookie.
10. Put cookie sheet in the oven and bake at 350°F for 10 minutes.

BELLA CHICKEN MARBELLA

PREP 10 mins

COOK 60 mins

SERVES 10

INGREDIENTS

- ☐ 4 chickens, 2½ pounds each, quartered
- ☐ 1 head garlic, peeled and finely pureed
- ☐ 1/4 cup dried oregano
- ☐ Course salt and freshly ground pepper, to taste
- ☐ 1/4 cup red wine vinegar
- ☐ 1/4 cup chicken stock
- ☐ 1/2 cup olive oil
- ☐ 1 cup prunes, pitted
- ☐ 1/2 cup spanish green olives, pitted
- ☐ 1/2 cup capers with a bit of juice
- ☐ 6 bay leaves
- ☐ 1 cup brown sugar
- ☐ 1 cup white wine
- ☐ 1/4 cup Italian parsley or fresh coriander (cilantro), finely chopped

INSTRUCTIONS

1. Preheat over to 350°F.
2. In a large bowl combine chicken quarters, garlic, oregano, pepper and coarse salt to taste, olive oil, prunes, olives, capers and juice, and bay leaves. Cover and let marinate, refrigerate overnight.
3. Arrange chicken in a single layer in one or two large, shallow baking pans and spoon marinade over it evenly. Sprinkle chicken pieces with brown sugar and pour white wine around them.
4. Bake for 50 minutes to 1 hour, basting frequently with pan juices. Chicken is done when thigh pieces, pricked with a fork at their thickest, yield clear yellow (rather than pink) juice.
5. With a slotted spoon transfer chicken, prunes, olives and capers to a serving platter. Moisten with a few spoonfuls of pan juices and sprinkle generously with parsley or cilantro. Pass remaining pan juices in a sauceboat.
6. To service Chicken Marbella cold, cool to room temperature in cooking juices before transferring to a serving platter. If chicken has been covered and refrigerated, allow it to return to room temperature before serving.

KERI

I am a single mom of two beautiful children below 5 years of age! I am always looking to find things that are quick and easy, yet full of flavours and vegetables that I know my kids will enjoy so I won't have to fight them to eat! I have spent my life watching my mother own the kitchen and continue to put beautiful meals out for our family and guests alike. Now that I've been in my kitchen trying to follow her footsteps for my family, I've been stealing some of her quick, delicious and presentable dishes! I hope that you will enjoy these favourite dishes of mine as much as my family does! Get Cooking!

HIGHER
THAN THE
MOUNTAINS

CRAZY CRANBERRY CHICKEN DINNER

PREP 20 mins

COOK 30 mins

SERVES 4-6

INGREDIENTS

- ☐ 4-6 chicken breasts
- ☐ 1/2 of each red, orange and yellow peppers
- ☐ Handful or two of green beans
- ☐ 1 can cranberry sauce
- ☐ 1/2 bottle russian salad dressing
- ☐ 1 package onion soup mix
- ☐ Oregano to taste
- ☐ Extra virgin olive oil

1

In a bowl mix together cranberry sauce, onion soup mix and russian salad dressing, stir until evenly mixed.

2

Place 4 to 6 chicken breasts in a baking dish and cover each of them with the mixed dressing. Be sure to lift each breast to allow the sauce to get underneath.

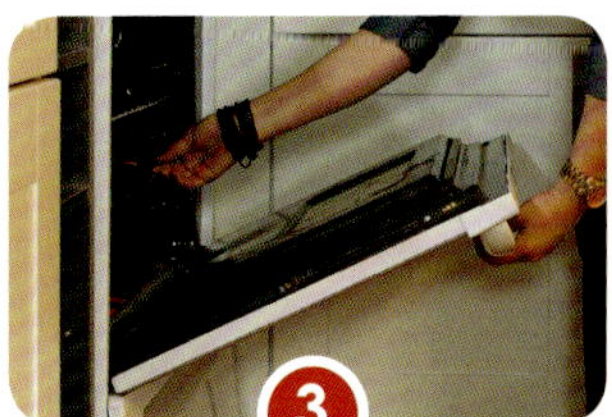

3

Preheat oven to 350°F then bake for 30 minutes or until chicken is fully cooked throughout.

4

Wash and slice the peppers lengthwise thinly, then set aside.

5

Wash green beans and set aside with peppers.

6

Add the green beans first with a splash of water to help steam them. Let sit for a couple minutes as they will take longer to cook then the peppers.

7

Then add the peppers with another splash of water.

8

After they soften slightly, add a little bit of extra virgin olive oil (just a few drizzles), a teaspoon of oregano, and some sea salt and cracked pepper. Ideally, you want to keep a little bit of crunch to the vegetables to keep the crispness.

9

Remove chicken from oven to cool and plate each breast with some vegetables.

If you wish, cook some Jasmine rice to accompany this meal, the extra sauce from the chicken makes for a great gravy like sauce for the rice.

THAI FLY LUCKY CHICKEN

PREP 5 mins

COOK 25 mins

SERVES 4-6

INGREDIENTS

- ☐ 4 chicken breasts
- ☐ 1 orange pepper
- ☐ 1 red pepper
- ☐ Any preferred vegetable your family enjoys
- ☐ 1 jar thai sweet chilli sauce (it is not spicy)
- ☐ 1-2 cups jasmine rice, or your preferred style of rice

INSTRUCTIONS

1. Add rice to your rice cooker slightly covering entire amount of rice with water.
2. Cube chicken breasts.
3. Chop peppers and vegetables.
4. Heat large frying pan or wok over medium heat; add chicken with a splash of water to replace using oil while cooking.
5. Cook chicken thoroughly until each cube is golden brown and all pink is removed from the meat.
6. Add peppers and vegetables with another splash of water to assist in steaming the vegetables you added. Let sit for a few minutes stirring occasionally so they don't stick to the frying pan.
7. Once vegetables soften slightly, add the entire jar of thai sweet chilli sauce stirring through the entire mixture of chicken and vegetables.
8. Remove from heat.
9. Place ½ cup or more of rice on each plate and then cover rice with your preferred amount of chicken mixture, also using surrounding sauce to soak through rice for extra flavouring.

IIP COCONUT SQUARES

PREP 10 mins

COOK 20 mins

SERVES 12

INGREDIENTS

- 1/2 cup softened or slightly melted butter
- 2 cups graham cracker crumbs
- 1 bag medium ground, unsweetened coconut
- 8 milk chocolate bars

INSTRUCTIONS

- Preheat oven to 350°F.
- Lightly grease glass baking dish.
- Mix together butter, graham crackers and coconut. Stir until everything is mixed and slightly moistened from the butter.
- Spread mix into the baking dish evenly. Place in oven for 20 minutes (or until mix is golden brown, as ovens may vary in cooking time).
- In a pot, or in a microwave, melt the chocolate bars until soft and spreadable (you may have to stir part way through heating to promote softening).
- Once the baking dish is done, remove from oven and spread the melted chocolate over the top of the baked mix.
- Let cool on the stove until it is safe to cover the dish and place into the fridge.
- Remove from fridge 30 to 60 minutes prior to preferred serving time allowing them to warm to room temperature for an easier cutting process.

LISA

I love to entertain and have a full bustling household, whether it is family, friends, or the neighbourhood kids. There is always something being cooked up, music playing in our kitchen and an impromptu dance party. I am also a lover of cheese. Friends who are lactose intolerant know to bring their pills so they still partake and not miss out on the scrumptious cheese creations.

These are some of my signature dishes my girlfriends have expected to be served when the wine starts flowing. The figs are inspired by a dish from one of our favourite Leslieville restaurant. I am always inspired when eating out around the city and love to put my own spin on the recipe.

Hot
Cooking

CHOCOLATE DRIZZLED
FIGS WITH MELTED GORGONZOLA

PREP 5 mins
COOK 10 mins
SERVES 6

INGREDIENTS

- ☐ 6 figs, cut in half
- ☐ 1/2 cup gorgonzola cheese
- ☐ 6 pieces dark chocolate with sea salt

1 Wash and cut figs in half. Place figs on baking dish.

2 Spread gorgonzola cheese on figs.

3 Bake in oven at 325°F for about 10 minutes or until cheese has melted and figs are baked.

4 While figs are in the oven, break up 6 pieces of dark chocolate and place in microwavable dish. Melt chocolate in microwave for 2 to 3 minutes or until fully melted.

5 Place baked figs on plate and drizzle dark chocolate over figs.

Any dark chocolate will work, however dark chocolate with sea salt will intensify the flavours and bring it to a new level.

BAKED BRIE WITH WALNUTS

PREP 5 mins

COOK 15 mins

SERVES 6

INGREDIENTS

- ☐ 1-200 gram round double cream brie
- ☐ 1 tablespoon brown sugar
- ☐ 1/4 cup walnut pieces
- ☐ 1 package mini toasts

1

Preheat oven to 350°F. Unwrap brie and place on cutting board. Cut brie into 8 pie like slices, only cutting about half way into the cheese.

2

Place brie into baking dish and sprinkle brown sugar and walnuts on top of cheese, pushing some of it into the cuts of the brie. Bake for about 15 minutes or until brie has melted.

3

Let cool at least 5 minutes before serving with mini toasts.

GOAT CHEESE WITH CARAMELIZED ONION AND PEAR BAGUETTE

PREP 15 mins

COOK 10 mins

SERVES 6

INGREDIENTS

- ☐ 1 fresh baguette
- ☐ 1/4 cup olive oil
- ☐ 1 sweet onion, finely sliced
- ☐ 1 pear, cored and thinly sliced
- ☐ 1 package goat cheese
- ☐ Pepper and salt to taste

1

Slice baguette into 1/2" thick pieces.

2

Dip both sides of bread into olive oil and place on baking sheet.

3

Bake in oven at 325°F for 5 minutes or until slightly golden.

4

Chop onions and pears and set aside.

5

On medium heat melt butter in skillet an
cook onion and pears until tender and
browned adding pepper and salt to tast

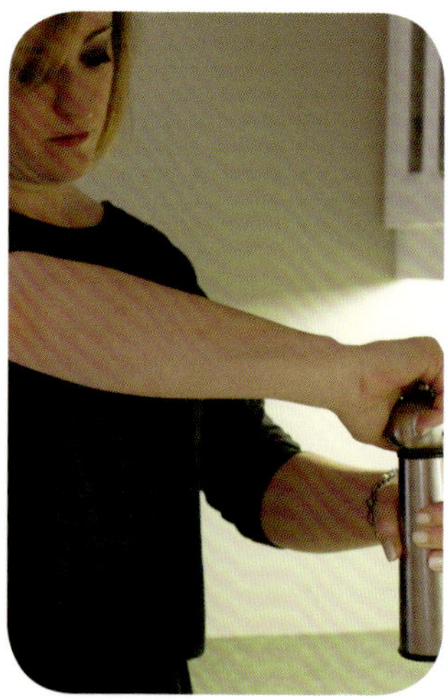

6

ke baguettes out of the oven and
ead a thick layer of goat cheese on
h slice. Pile caramelized onion and
rs on each slice and return to oven
for 5 minutes.

7

Place slices on plate and drizzle with olive oil.

SUBMISSIVE TENDERLION GORGONZOLA PROSCIUTTO & APRICOTS

PREP 10 mins
COOK 45 mins
SERVES 6

INGREDIENTS

- ☐ 2 pork tenderloins
- ☐ 1/2 cup gorgonzola cheese
- ☐ 5 slices prosciutto
- ☐ 1/2 cup walnuts or pecans
- ☐ 1/2 cup dried apricots
- ☐ 1 cup red wine
- ☐ Fresh parsley and sage
- ☐ Pepper and salt

INSTRUCTIONS

1. Preheat oven to 325°F.
2. Slice pork tenderloins through center without cutting through all the way and butterfly open.
3. Stuff tenderloins with gorgonzola, prosciutto, apricots and ¼ cup of nuts.
4. Fold tenderloins back together and place in cast iron dutch oven or other baking dish with lid.
5. Pepper and salt to taste and add fresh herbs.
6. Crush remaining nuts and sprinkle on top of tenderloins.
7. Pour wine over tenderloins, cover and place in oven.
8. Bake for 45 minutes, temperature of meat should reach 145°F.
9. Let it rest at least 5 minutes. Then slice into 1/2" thick pieces and serve.

WILD & BROWN RICE ROASTED BEETS

PREP 25 mins

COOK 1.5 hours

SERVES 6

INGREDIENTS

- ☐ 4 servings of brown and wild rice
- ☐ 4 roasted beets
- ☐ 3 roasted cloves of garlic
- ☐ 1/2 sweet onion, diced
- ☐ 1 carrot, diced
- ☐ 1/2 cup feta cheese
- ☐ 3 tablespoons white wine vinegar
- ☐ 2 tablespoons olive oil
- ☐ 1 tablespoon Dijon mustard
- ☐ Pepper and salt

INSTRUCTIONS

1. Cook 4 servings of brown and wild rice, as per packaging.
2. Preheat oven to 400°F.
3. Line baking dish with foil for easy clean up.
4. Place beets and garlic cloves in dish, drizzle with olive oil, and bake for 1 hour.
5. When cool, peel then dice beets and squeeze cloves to extract roasted garlic.
6. In a medium sized skillet, heat olive oil and saute sweet onion and carrots until fragrant.
7. In a large bowl, combine rice, beets, garlic, onion, carrots and feta cheese.
8. In a small bowl, whisk together vinegar, olive oil, mustard, pepper and salt.
9. Pour over rice dish and toss to coat.

TIP This dish can be served both hot and cold.

PATRICIA

I am a mom of two active boys aged 10 and 12. Eating healthy and being physically active is very important to me.
The boys play hockey, and this keeps me very busy, as well as my professional career and daily work out with the gym crew girls.
I enjoy mountain biking, and adventure racing throughout the year.

Growing up, chicken schnitzel was a favourite weekend meal for my brother and me. A fresh hot schnitzel would be served with rice and a side dish of steamed veggies or a cool salad. I fondly remember this meal from my childhood.
Now this is a favourite meal I serve to my own children.

CHICKEN BREAST SCHNITZEL
WITH MELTED CHEESE & SAUTEED MUSHROOMS

PREP 15 mins

COOK 30 mins

SERVES 6

INGREDIENTS

- ☐ 5 or 6 boneless/skinless chicken breasts
- ☐ 1½ cups seasoned bread crumbs
- ☐ 3 eggs, beaten
- ☐ 2½ cups cheese, shredded (marble or light cheddar)
- ☐ 4 cups mushrooms, sliced
- ☐ 1 tablespoon butter
- ☐ Oil for frying

1 Use a smooth sided mallet to tenderize the chicken breasts until they are a little less than a 1/4 inch thick.

2 Set up three wide, shallow bowls for the flour, eggs and bread crumbs. (Have a large plate ready for placing the coated schnitzels).

3 Dip and coat each breast, first in flour, eggs, then bread crumbs.

4 Pour oil into a skillet until it is deep enough for frying (approximately 1/2 inch). Heat the oil slowly over medium heat; when hot enough for frying, place the coated breast in a single layer until they are golden brown (approximately 3 to 4 minutes each).

5 Remove onto baking sheet covered with parchment paper, set aside and start on the mushrooms.

6

Heat 1 tablespoon of butter in a pan over medium heat. Saute the sliced mushrooms 3 to 4 minutes or until starting to brown.

While mushrooms are cooking...

7

Distribute the shredded cheese evenly among the chicken schnitzels on the baking sheet.

8

Heat the broiler of your oven to 400°F and place the baking sheet for 3 to 4 minutes or until the cheese has nicely bubbled and is melted.

9

Once cheese has melted, turn off heat and remove from oven. Distribute mushrooms on the chicken schnitzels. Transfer the schnitzels to your serving dish and serve.

COOL BROCCOLI SALAD

PREP 20 mins

COOK 1-2 hours

SERVES 4

INGREDIENTS

- ☐ 6 cups small broccoli florets
- ☐ 3/4 cup cranrasins
- ☐ 1/2 cup almonds, slivered
- ☐ 1/2 cup unsalted sunflower seeds, roasted
- ☐ 1/3 cup green onions, chopped
- ☐ 1 cup crispy bacon crumble
- ☐ 1 cup triple cheddar cheese mix, shredded
- ☐ 1 cup mayonnaise

INSTRUCTIONS

1. Combine broccoli, cranraisins, slivered almonds, sunflower seeds in large bowl.
2. Add mayonnaise; toss to coat.
3. Refrigerate 1 to 2 hours.
4. Sprinkle with crispy bacon crumble before serving.

TIP I like to microwave bacon in paper towel layers to make it crispy.

RASPBERRY/AVOCADO SPINACH SALAD

PREP 15 mins

COOK 0 mins

SERVES 2-4

INGREDIENTS

- ☐ 1 pound fresh baby spinach
- ☐ 2 cups raspberries
- ☐ 1 cup avocado chunks
- ☐ 1/2 cup almonds, slivered

DRESSING

- ☐ 1/4 cup raspberry vinegar
- ☐ 1/2 cup light olive oil
- ☐ 1½ tablespoons poppy seeds
- ☐ 1½ tablespoons brown sugar
- ☐ 1/4 teaspoon paprika
- ☐ 1 teaspoon dry mustard
- ☐ 1/4 teaspoon Worcestershire sauce
- ☐ 2 teaspoons onion, finely chopped

INSTRUCTIONS

1. Combine ALL dressing ingredients in a container with a tight fitting lid.
2. Shake well to blend.
3. Place spinach & raspberries in a large bowl. Add dressing & toss.
4. Add almonds. Serve immediately.

SUE

My goal in the past 2 years was to get healthy and get back in top notch shape. Looking at me you might wonder what the heck I was talking about, due to my decent figure. But it wasn't my body that needed fixing, it was my mind. I've always believed if you take care of your body then your body will take care of you. Mentally you must figure out what drives you, what is your passion, what makes you feel good... For me that is working out and eating well, and that's what I've been doing. The eating well part translates into one of my passions which is cooking. I love to create new dishes. I don't have any formal training, but what I do have is an imagination and a flare for flavours. I've owned my own restaurant and catering company before which allowed me lots of hours in the kitchen developing my talent. I hope you enjoy the tasty dishes I have created.

KALE & CHICKEN DELIGHT

PREP 10 mins

COOK 35 mins

SERVES 2

INGREDIENTS

- ☐ 1 tablespoon coconut oil
- ☐ 1 cup cremini mushrooms, sliced
- ☐ 1 medium red onion, sliced in half rings
- ☐ 1 cup cooked chicken, chopped
- ☐ 1 cup fresh cut carrot slaw
- ☐ 6 kale stalks, remove stalks
- ☐ 1/2 tablespoon sesame seeds
- ☐ 1 clove garlic

1 Wash and slice mushrooms and onions.

2 Put coconut oil in large frying pan or wok, set stove top to medium to high heat.
Add sliced mushrooms, saute for 10 minutes.
Add onion, continue to saute for another 10 minutes.

3 Add chicken, mix well.

4 Add carrot slaw, mix well, saute for another 10 minutes.

5

Break kale into pieces and add to the mix, continue stirring for another 5 minutes. Remove from heat.

5 Place on plates, sprinkle with sesame seeds.

LATE NIGHT BREAKFAST BONANZA

PREP 20 mins

COOK 50 mins

SERVES 6

INGREDIENTS

- ☐ 3 medium ripe bananas
- ☐ 1/2 cup buttermilk
- ☐ 3/4 cup coconut oil
- ☐ 1 cup brown sugar
- ☐ 1 egg
- ☐ 1 teaspoon vanilla
- ☐ 1½ teaspoons baking soda
- ☐ 1½ teaspoons baking powder
- ☐ 2¼ cups spelt flour
- ☐ 1/4 teaspoon salt

INSTRUCTIONS

1. Preheat oven set to 350°F.
2. With mixer, beat bananas until mashed.
3. Add milk, coconut oil & sugar, mix until smooth.
4. Add egg and vanilla, beat to mix.
5. Add flour, baking soda, baking powder & salt. Beat until well mixed.
6. Prepare baking dish by spraying with non-stick spray, then lightly dusting with flour. Pour mixture into bread loaf pan.
7. Bake for 50 minutes.
8. Let cool before cutting.

SUE'S LUNCH MUNCH

PREP 10 mins

COOK 0 mins

SERVES 1

INGREDIENTS

- ☐ 1 can solid tuna
- ☐ 1 large tomato
- ☐ 1 medium cucumber
- ☐ 1 hard boiled egg
- ☐ 1 avocado
- ☐ 2 tablespoons balsamic vinegar
- ☐ 2 tablespoons olive oil
- ☐ Sea salt and pepper

INSTRUCTIONS

1. Drain tuna, and break into very small pieces in bowl.
2. Dice tomato into medium bite size cubes add to bowl.
3. Dice cucumber, add to bowl.
4. Dice egg, add to bowl.
5. Dice avocado, add to bowl.
6. Add balsamic vinegar, oil, salt & pepper. Mix well.
7. Let stand for 5 minutes, stir again and serve.

REAL MOMS COOKING REAL FOOD

RECIPES BY REAL MOMS

Love to Cook? Hate to Cook? Doesn't really matter. Eventually you have to eat...

More than just a cookbook, Hot Moms Cookbook is a testament to Moms conviction that anything is possible in today's world - with the right mix of persistence and innovative thinking. This cookbook is a journey featuring real moms in their own kitchens. These moms reveal a glimpse into the inner workings of an average mom cooking up a family meal.

A fresh new attitude to cooking.

There is no right or wrong way to cook, only a fun way! Hot Moms Cookbook was created to promote adventurous home cooked meals and to change the way we think about cooking.

Here are a few more moms that wanted to share their personal recipes with you. If you would like to see more and share yours as well, please visit us at www.hotmomscooking.com

CAULIFLOWER / BROCCOLI PITTULE

INGREDIENTS

- 1 cup flour
- 1 medium broccoli or cauliflower
- 4 tablespoons parmesan cheese, grated
- 4-5 sprigs fresh parsley
- 1 clove garlic, minced
- 2 eggs
- 1/2 cup water
- Vegetable oil for frying
- Salt and pepper to taste

INSTRUCTIONS

- Mix flour, eggs, garlic, parsley, black pepper and salt.
- Add water slowly until it resembles a pancake like texture.
- In salted water, boil broccoli or cauliflower.
- Heat oil in fry pan.
- Dip broccoli or cauliflower in batter and fry.
- Place on paper towel to drain extra oil, serve warm.

TERESA MICIELI

FAVOURITE PUMPKIN ROLL

INGREDIENTS

- ☐ 3 eggs
- ☐ 1 cup pumpkin puree
- ☐ 1 teaspoon baking soda
- ☐ 1/2 teaspoon salt
- ☐ 1 tablespoon cinnamon
- ☐ 3/4 cup flour

FILLING

- ☐ 8 ounces cream cheese
- ☐ 1 teaspoon vanilla
- ☐ 2 tablespoons butter
- ☐ 1 cup icing sugar

INSTRUCTIONS

1. Beat eggs, add baking soda, salt, and then pumpkin a little bit at a time; add cinnamon then flour a little bit at a time. Line a cookie sheet with wax paper, spray with cooking spray. Pour batter evenly on a cookie sheet and bake at 375°F for 15 minutes.
2. Remove from oven and place on a tea towel, pull off wax paper and roll cake onto a tea towel to cool.

FILLING

1. Mix cream cheese, butter, vanilla and icing sugar until smooth. Once cake is cooled, roll open and spread the filling evenly from corner to corner. Gently roll up the cake, wrap with cling wrap and refrigerate for 3 hours.
2. Before serving remove cling wrap and sprinkle with icing sugar.

LINA GRANDE

CITRUS SALMON FILLETS

INGREDIENTS

- ☐ 4 salmon fillets
- ☐ 3 tablespoons extra virgin olive oil
- ☐ 1½ tablespoons fresh squeezed lemon juice
- ☐ 1 tablespoon fresh squeezed orange juice
- ☐ 1/2 teaspoon lemon zest
- ☐ 1/2 teaspoon orange rind
- ☐ 1 teaspoon honey
- ☐ 1/2 teaspoon ginger, minced
- ☐ 1/2 teaspoon fresh thyme, chopped
- ☐ 1/2 teaspoon fresh parsley, chopped
- ☐ 1/2 teaspoon onion powder
- ☐ 1 teaspoon garlic powder
- ☐ 1/2 teaspoon black pepper
- ☐ 1/2 teaspoon sea salt
- ☐ Orange and lemon slices to top fillets

INSTRUCTIONS

1. Add all marinade ingredients to a bowl and whisk to combine.
2. Place salmon fillets in a ziploc bag, pour marinade over to fully coat fish and place in fridge to marinate for 45 minutes.
3. Preheat oven to 350°F.
4. Place salmon on baking sheet and top each fillet with a slice of lemon and orange, if you like.
5. Bake for 40 minutes or to desired doneness.

ROSIE FERREIRA

KING QABELI PALAU

INGREDIENTS

- ☐ 2 cups rice, long grained (4-5 hours in advance)
- ☐ 1/2 kilogram lamb
- ☐ 1/3 cup ghee
- ☐ Salt to taste
- ☐ 1½ tablespoons, rice spices (cloves, cumin, cardamom, cinnamon)
- ☐ 3 tablespoons soya sauce
- ☐ 2 cups carrots, julienned
- ☐ 1/2 cup raisins
- ☐ 1/4 cup almonds, blanched
- ☐ 1/4 cup pistachio, blanched
- ☐ 1 tablespoon sugar
- ☐ Oil for frying

INSTRUCTIONS

1. Cook the meat in 2 cups of salted water for 20 minutes.
2. Fry julienned carrots for 6 minutes, raisins for 2 minutes, almonds and pistachios for 2 minutes one by one in oil. Remove from oil and place separately in foil. Sprinkle a tablespoon of sugar on them and wrap. Set aside.
3. Remove the meat from the broth, take half a cup of broth then add rice spices, salt, soya sauce and set aside.
4. Get the rice that you have washed and soaked at least 4 to 5 hours in advance.
5. Boil the rice in the water and salt, do not over cook it. Remove from heat and drain.
6. Add a tablespoon of oil then pour the rice into the cooking pot, place the meat in the center of rice and cover it with the rice. Now slowly pour soup mixture to the rice. To avoid the breakage of rice make holes in the rice by using the back of the spatula. Place carrots, raisins, almonds, pistachios on one side of the rice too.
7. Cover the pot with cotton cloth and let it steam and cook for 20 minutes on very low heat.
8. Heat ghee and pour it all over the rice and cook for 5 more minutes.
9. When the rice is cooked first remove the raisins, almonds, carrots, pistachios and meat from the rice. Place the meat in a large plate then cover it with rice, spread carrots, raisins, almonds and pistachios on top of rice. Ready to serve.

MUSKA NAIKZAD

PICANHA MADE IN BRAZIL

INGREDIENTS

- ☐ 1 tablespoon unsalted butter
- ☐ 1½ cups of shiitake mushrooms
- ☐ 1 piece of picanha - apply coarse salt to taste
- ☐ 1½ cups of mini onions
- ☐ 1½ cups of cooked mini potatoes
- ☐ 1 zucchini, sliced

INSTRUCTIONS

1. Remove the stems of shiitake mushrooms.
2. Put them to soak in water for about 20 minutes.
3. Drain the water, chop and set aside.
4. In a grill pan, place the butter and brown the steak and sprinkle the coarse salt (to taste).
5. Turn it several times, until it reaches your desired point.
6. On the same grill, brown the mushrooms, mini onions, potatoes and zucchini.
7. Serve with the picanha.

TIP The picanha can also be served with white rice.

TANIA CARABETTA VIEIRA DIAS

COD FISH BACCALA BALLS

INGREDIENTS

- ☐ 2 pieces of dried, boneless cod fish
- ☐ 2 green onions, chopped
- ☐ 2 yellow potatoes, boiled
- ☐ 1/2 cup parsley, chopped
- ☐ Vegetable oil for frying
- ☐ Salt to taste

INSTRUCTIONS

1. Soak cod fish for 3 days, changing water daily.
2. Boil cod fish for approximately 4 to 5 minutes.
3. Boil potatoes.
4. Put cod fish and potatoes in food processor and blend until it is a chunky consistency.
5. Remove mixture from processor and place in a bowl.
6. Add onions, parsley and salt to taste.
7. Shape mixture into 2 to 3 inch balls, or desired size.
8. Fry balls in vegetable oil, either on stove top in a deep pan or in a deep fryer until golden brown.
9. Deep fryer temperature should be at least 350°F.

DORA MIOLLA

FAMOUS
ASIAN STIR-FRY VEGETABLES

INGREDIENTS

- ☐ 4 teaspoons butter
- ☐ 1 clove garlic, chopped
- ☐ 2 teaspoons orange peel, grated
- ☐ 1/2 teaspoon fresh ginger, grated
- ☐ 1 tablespoon green onion, chopped
- ☐ 1 teaspoon Asian chili sauce (sriracha) or hot pepper sauce
- ☐ 1 pound assorted fresh vegetables (Chinese greens, broccoli, onions, snow peas, green and/or red pepper and carrots)

INSTRUCTIONS

1. Heat butter in a large non-stick wok or skillet over medium to high heat.
2. Saute assorted fresh vegetables, stirring frequently, about 5 minutes or until crisp tender.
3. Combine, green onion, orange peel, ginger, garlic and chilli sauce in a large bowl then add to the wok or skillet mix for 1 minute.
4. Serve on a bed of steamed white rice.

DEBORAH WU

ROASTED CHERRY TOMATOES WITH RICOTTA ON CROSTINI

INGREDIENTS

- ☐ 2 cups yellow cherry tomatoes
- ☐ 2 cups red cherry tomatoes
- ☐ 4 tablespoons extra virgin olive oil
- ☐ 1 teaspoon white sugar
- ☐ 2 teaspoons coarse pink Himalayan salt
- ☐ 1 clove garlic, finely minced
- ☐ 250 grams ricotta cheese
- ☐ Handful fresh basil leaves roughly chopped
- ☐ 1 French baguette sliced into 1/2″ thick slices

INSTRUCTIONS

1. Preheat your oven to 400°F.
2. Slice tomatoes in half and place in mixing bowl.
3. Sprinkle tomatoes with sugar, toss and let sit for a few minutes, (it brings out their sweetness). Then add 1/2 tablespoon of olive oil, basil, garlic, salt and toss again.
4. Place tomatoes in a parchment-lined glass baking dish and roast in oven for 35 to 45 minutes until they are bursting.
5. While tomatoes are roasting, brush baguette slices lightly on each side with remaining olive oil. Place on parchment lined baking sheet and bake for 8 to 10 minutes, (or until they turn golden) turning once half-way through.
6. To finish: spread ricotta on warm crostini, then spoon a tablespoon of tomatoes on top with a drizzle of the jus.

JENNIFER EISEN

GOAT CHEESE MASHED CAULIFLOWER

INGREDIENTS

- ☐ 1 large cauliflower (stems and florets cut into bite size pieces
- ☐ 1/2 cup soft goat cheese
- ☐ 1 tablespoon milk
- ☐ 1/2 teaspoon salt
- ☐ 1/4 teaspoon pepper
- ☐ 1/4 teaspoon dried oregano
- ☐ 1/4 teaspoon parsley
- ☐ 1/4 teaspoon garlic powder
- ☐ 1 tablespoon extra virgin olive oil

INSTRUCTIONS

1. In a steamer, (or steam basket) steam the cauliflower for about 10 minutes or until tender.
2. Once ready, place cauliflower in a bowl and use a potato masher to mash cauliflower just until it has the texture of mashed potatoes.
3. Add the goat cheese, milk, salt, pepper and other spices. Stir until all combined.
4. Add 1 tablespoon of extra virgin olive oil in a casserole and spread mashed cauliflower in it.
5. Bake at 350°F for 10 to 12 minutes.

KEILBASA POTATOES

INGREDIENTS

- ☐ 7-8 large potatoes
- ☐ 7-8 eggs
- ☐ 2-3 dry smoked sausages (or kielbasa)
- ☐ 2 cups sour cream
- ☐ Salt and pepper to taste

INSTRUCTIONS

1. Boil potatoes with skin on until almost cooked.
2. As you are boiling the potatoes, also hard boil the eggs.
3. Cut up the dry sausage or kielbasa.
4. Mix the sour cream with some salt.
5. Peel and slice both potatoes and eggs, as if you were making a potato salad or scalloped potatoes.
6. Grease a pan with some olive oil.
7. Layer with potatoes first followed by eggs, sausage and a thin-ish layer of sour cream.
8. Repeat the layers. All extra sour cream should be put on the last layer (potato). There should be enough to cover it with at least an inch thickness. If not, use more sour cream! Decide how hardy you want to make this dish. The more quantity you use, the tastier the potatoes will be!
9. Bake at 350°F for approximately 30 minutes, until the sour cream mixture starts to brown.
10. Serve hot with a simple green salad.

MARIJANA MANCE

FRIDAY NIGHT CHICKEN SPECIAL

INGREDIENTS

- ☐ 1 whole chicken uncooked (giblets removed)
- ☐ Salt and pepper to taste
- ☐ 1 teaspoon paprika
- ☐ 1/2 tablespoon extra virgin olive oil
- ☐ 4 cloves fresh garlic, chopped
- ☐ 1-2 tablespoons barbeque chicken seasoning
- ☐ 2 tablespoons fresh basil, chopped

INSTRUCTIONS

1. Preheat the oven to 375°F.
2. Spray a foil tray or cooking dish with cooking spray.
3. Wash the whole chicken and put it directly into the dish (don't pat it dry, you want a little water to be in the tray).
4. Once the chicken is in the dish, add the salt, pepper, paprika and olive oil to the chicken. Massage it all around.
5. Pour the seasoning on top of the chicken. Rub it inside and outside of the chicken. You want a generous amount on it.
6. Add garlic and basil to the chicken.
7. Cover the tray or dish with foil tightly.
8. Bake the chicken in the oven for 55 minutes.
9. Take out the chicken and remove the foil. Put it on broil for 3 to 4 minutes on each side so the outside is crispy.
10. Put on a plate and it is ready to serve.

JENNIFER STALLMAN

FARFALLE WITH ZUCCHINI FLOWERS

INGREDIENTS

- ☐ 4 tablespoons Colavita extra virgin olive oil
- ☐ 4 ounces of white wine
- ☐ 10 zucchini flowers, diced
- ☐ Half a zucchini
- ☐ 200 grams lean pancetta, diced
- ☐ 1 small pearl onion, diced
- ☐ 1 clove garlic, crushed
- ☐ 4 to 5 leaves fresh basil
- ☐ Parmesan cheese, grated
- ☐ 1pack Molisana farfalle pasta

INSTRUCTIONS

1. In a sauce pan, add the onion, olive oil and garlic. Saute until the onion is golden.
2. Add the pancetta and continue to saute over gentle heat.
3. Add the zucchini, after a couple of minutes add the zucchini flowers.
4. Continue to saute, add white wine.
5. Add basil whole or diced, your preference.
6. Remove from heat.
7. Boil your pasta in salted water to an al dente consistency.
8. Add sauce, mix and place in pasta bowls.
9. Garnish with basil and parmesan cheese.

TERESA DIBIASE

MAPLE CURRY CHICKEN PENNE

INGREDIENTS

- ☐ 2 tablespoons olive oil
- ☐ 2 tablespoons butter
- ☐ 1 large onion, chopped
- ☐ 1 red bell pepper
- ☐ 2 cups cooked chicken breast, cubed
- ☐ 3 cloves garlic
- ☐ 3 green onions or chives
- ☐ 1 teaspoon sugar
- ☐ 1/4 cup maple syrup
- ☐ 1 cup heavy cream
- ☐ 2½ tablespoons curry paste or powder
- ☐ 1 box penne pasta, cooked and drained
- ☐ 4 ounces cream cheese, cubed

INSTRUCTIONS

1. Heat butter and oil in a skillet.
2. Add onions and peppers over medium heat.
3. Cook until the onions become translucent (usually 6 to 7 minutes).
4. Stir in chicken and garlic and sprinkle with the sugar.
5. Cook for another 3 or 4 minutes.
6. Then stir in maple syrup and cook for another 5 or 6 minutes or until carmelized.
7. Stir in the curry paste (or powder) and cream cheese and reduce the heat to low.
8. Simmer uncovered for about 15 minutes to let the flavours mix.
9. Add cream and simmer until smooth.
10. Mix with the penne and sprinkle with green onion.

NANCY DELANO

WHO WILL BE THE NEXT HOT MOM?

SCOOTING ACROSS CANADA TO FIND OUT

Join us on our next adventure of tempting new recipes and flavours. Inspired by the exceptional foods found in the ordinary homes of real moms. We are positive they will pique your culinary curiosity and help you turn regular ingredients into amazing meals. This unique cookbook will feature a wide range of recipes that utilize a variety of ingredients. There's no shortage of healthy and great tasting meal ideas here - Hot Moms Cookbook - HOT & SPICY will be packed full with recipes by regular moms. The recipes don't require a great deal of experience in the kitchen, which makes them great for novice cooks or just the tired mom looking for a quick and tasty dinner idea.